THE LETTERS OF JOHN

~ In this we know love ~

José Young

Ediciones Crecimiento Cristiano

Young, José
    The letters of John : In this we know love / José Young. - 1a ed. - Villa Nueva :
Crecimiento Cristiano, 2020.
    56 p. ; 21 x 14 cm.

    Traducción de: José Young.
    ISBN 978-987-1219-45-2

    1. Estudios Bíblicos. I. Título.
    CDD 226.506

This study is a translation of "Las cartas de Juan: Así conocemos el amor" published by Ediciones Crecimiento Cristiano, Villa Nueva, Argentina, [I.S.B.N. 978-987-1219-44-5]

1ª Edición inglés: Octubre 2020
ISBN: 978-987-1219-44-5

Córdoba 419 - Villa Nueva - Cba. - Argentina

+54 9 353 491-2450

+54 9 353 481-0724

oficina@edicionescc.com

www.edicionescc.com

Ediciones Crecimiento Cristiano

edicionescc

Index

4 ~ The letters of John

FIRST JOHN

6 ~ The letters of John

Introduction

The manner in that God showed his love is very clear. It is he who took the initiative and he who sent Jesus to the cross to give us life.

But what proof do we give that we really love God? That is what we will be exploring as we work through the pages of this letter.

When we begin to read 1 John we can see at once the style of his gospel: simple, but profound. With his repetitive style, he says a lot with few words.

It is calculated that the letter was written around the year 95 and that its principal purpose was to combat the Gnostic heresy. Gnosticism promoted a separation of the material from the spiritual. For them, the material was bad and the "spiritual" was good. They even arrived at the extreme position of denying that Christ was really human. To them Christ lived in the body of the human Jesus like a shell, a spiritual being hidden in a human body.

The Gnostic heresy had both doctrinal and practical consequences and John spends a good part of his letter combating them.

During the study I may make reference to three versions of the Bible:

RSV - Revised Standard Version
NIV - New International Version
ESV - English Standard Version

8 ~ The letters of John

1   Life and Light

1 John 1:1-10

Without any introduction John goes directly to his topic. It is a notable contrast to the custom of society and Paul's practice.

1- When John says: "That which was from the beginning...", what does he mean?

John and the other disciples had a privileged relationship with the Lord. Can you imagine what it would be like to hear him personally and to even touch him?

2- What do 1 Peter 1:8 and 2 Corinthians 5:16 say about verse 1?

Both in his gospel and in this letter, John speaks of the "word" of life.

3- What does the use of "word" to refer to the Lord tell us about him?

John began his gospel very similarly to how he starts this letter.
4- What do we learn about the "word" in John 1:1-14?

The word became flesh and his disciples heard him. That they heard him was evidence. Seeing him was even stronger evidence. But the fact that they touched him was the secure proof that the word became flesh and lived among us.

John writes as a witness, and makes his announcement with authority. He wrote so that those who read it could have fellowship with him and the other disciples. It is important to note that as John states, the purpose of his message was to create a relationship, to form a community. It is true that God offers life to each of us, but his purpose is the formation of a new creation, his church.

John's message is simple: "God is light".

5- Is it the same to say "God is light" as it is to say "God is like a light"? Why?

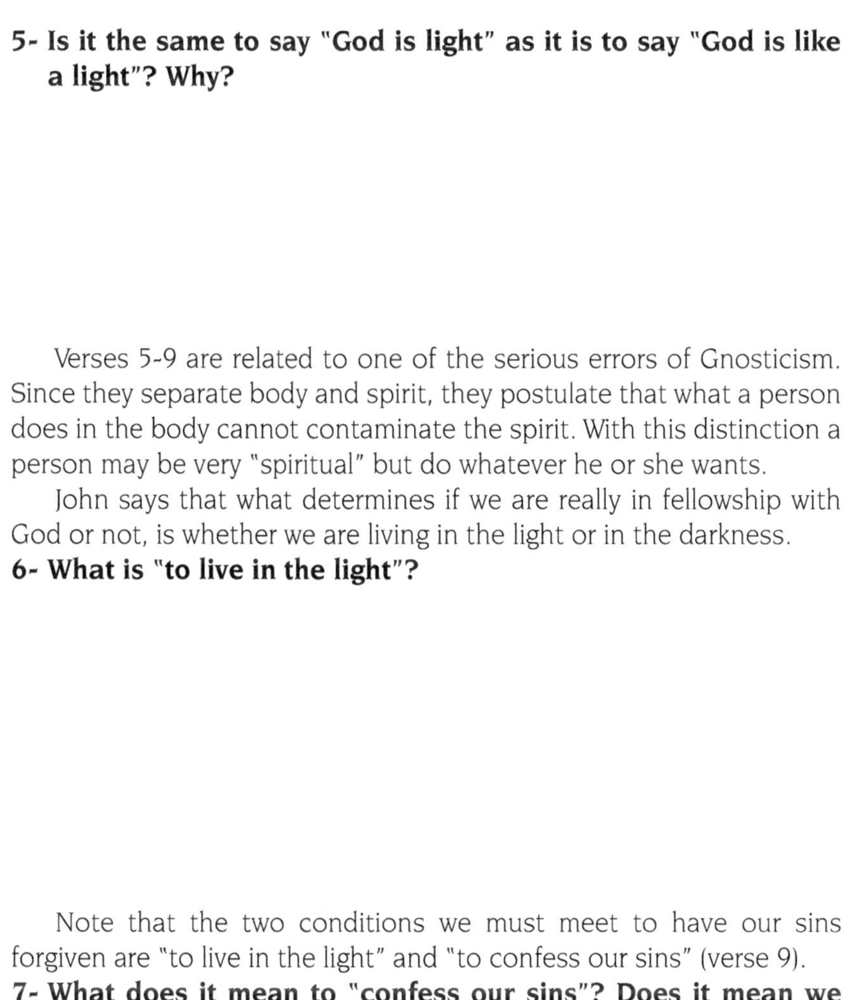

Verses 5-9 are related to one of the serious errors of Gnosticism. Since they separate body and spirit, they postulate that what a person does in the body cannot contaminate the spirit. With this distinction a person may be very "spiritual" but do whatever he or she wants.

John says that what determines if we are really in fellowship with God or not, is whether we are living in the light or in the darkness.

6- **What is "to live in the light"?**

Note that the two conditions we must meet to have our sins forgiven are "to live in the light" and "to confess our sins" (verse 9).

7- **What does it mean to "confess our sins"? Does it mean we should make a list of all the wrong things we do during the day and read it before God? Or is it something different?**

I am sure that none of us would pretend that we never have sinned.

8- What is the difference between "being sinful" and "committing sins"?

John says that it is a mistake to "say we have no sin" (verse 8), but we have a problem with Paul in Romans 6:2 when he says we have "died to sin".

9- How do we understand verse 8 in the light of Romans 6:2?

What should encourage us from verse 9 is that God not only forgives but also cleanses. He forgives us, but also works in our lives to eliminate the causes.

John affirms that if we confess our sins God is faithful and just to forgive our sins. He is faithful because he has promised it. He is just because Jesus Christ paid the account of even the most miserable sinner.

Old and new

1 John 2:1-17

John says that he has written this letter so that we may not sin. But at the same time, he recognizes our weakness and that we are very far from being perfect. He continues saying that if we sin, we have a solution. In most versions of the Bible in verse 1 he is called an "advocate". Though the same word in the RSV and ESV (John 14:16) is translated "helper" and "counselor".

1- How can that word help us understand verse 1?

2- If the sacrifice of Christ on the cross brings us forgiveness of sins, why is it necessary to have an advocate?

In verse 2 there is a key word that different versions of the Bible translate differently. John says that Christ is:

- the expiation for our sins. (RSV)
- the propitiation for our sins. (ESV)
- the atoning sacrifice for our sins. (NIV)

3- How do Psalms 7:11, Psalms 78:38 and Romans 1:18 help us clarify verse 2?

4- Does verse 2 imply that all humanity will be saved?

In the original Greek version of the New Testament verse 2 starts with: "By this means we know...", and it is an expression that John repeats some 25 times in one form or another. He presents proofs so that we may know that a person who professes to be a Christian really is one or not. But verses 3 to 6 create a bit of a problem, since there are many believers in our churches about whom it would be difficult to say that they obey God.

5- What does "to obey God" really mean? To what extreme are we to apply it?

6- Are verses 3 to 6 an adequate measure to know if a person really is of God?

7- How do we evaluate ourselves if we take these verses literally?

8- Looking at verses 7 to 9,
   a) What is the old commandment that at the same time is new?

   b) If it is old, in what manner is it new?

In verse 8 we return to the illustration of "light". We often find these themes of light and darkness in the New Testament.

9- There is a clear parallel between physical light and spiritual light.

a) If we remain in the light there is less chance of stumbling. How do we apply that to the Christian life?

b) If we walk in the light, we can see our goal. How do we apply that to the Christian life?

It's important to note that both Jesus and John insist in the contrast of light and darkness. They don't talk about "shadows" or partial light. It is light or dark, white or black, yes or no.

In verses 12 to 14 John speaks of three groups: children, young men and fathers. He is not referring to physical ages, but spiritual ages, the same we would normally encounter in a church.

10- What characteristics would you expect of each spiritual age? Don't limit you answer to this passage.

a) Children

b) Young men

c) Fathers

"Do not love the world" is an exhortation we find time after time in the New Testament. We cannot love God and at the same time love the world. We have a jealous God (Exodus 34:14)

11- John mentions three aspects of this world that we shouldn't love. Explain what they would be in our present day.

  a) "The desires of the flesh." (ESV); "The lust of the flesh." (RSV); "The cravings of sinful man." (NIV)

  b) "The desires of the eyes." (ESV); "The lust of the eyes." (RSV)

  c) "Pride in possessions." (ESV); "The pride of life." (RSV); "The boasting of what he has and does." (NIV)

And the world passes away. But John does not say it will pass away, but that it is passing (Note the ESV)

12- If then John is speaking of the present, what could he mean? What is passing away?

We live surrounded by darkness. We live in a world that is against God's purposes. What John proposes is life.

"And now, little children, abide in him..." (2:28)

3   The liar

1 John 2:18-27

Jesus said that he would return, but didn't say when (Mark 13:32). Christians during the first century thought it would be during their lifetime, just as Christians believe today.

But John introduces a new theme: the antichrist. The word can mean either of two things: "he who opposes Christ" or "he who pretends to take the place of Christ." Antichrist is a word that only appears in John's letters. And in the context of his letters, it is probable that it describes those who oppose Christ, who reject him in some way.

1- What more do we learn of them from 1 John 4:3 and 2 John 7?

2- It is very possible that the antichrist is the same "being" mentioned in 2 Thessalonians 2:1-12. How do these verses help us understand who the antichrist is and what he is like?

John says that he will come at a later date but that there were already many with his essence (see 4:3). If there were "antichrists" in John's time, they surely must exist now.

3- If that is so, what are they like? Who would they be?

John says that the antichrists of his day had left the church. He doesn't say whether they formed their own church or not, just that they simply left.

4- Is there a similar situation in our churches? Explain your answer.

It is sure, as John says, that the person who professes to be a Christian but denies that Jesus is the Christ is a liar.

5- From your experience, what other "liars" could we have in our churches?

The "anointing" mentioned in verse 20 refers to the oil used to set apart a priest or king. It was normally applied to the person's head. A good example is Exodus 29:7 that speaks of anointing a priest.

6- If we take into account John 14:26 and 2 Corinthians 1:21, 22, what would that anointing be?

John states that the person who has the "anointing" knows the truth (verse 21).

7- Does that mean that we know enough and do not need to study the Bible? Explain your answer.

There were some people who denied that Jesus was the Christ. That is, they said that the man Jesus and the Christ were two different persons. According to their belief, the Christ came upon Jesus at his baptism and left before the crucifixion. Verse 23 tells the consequences.

8- How can we avoid being led astray (verse 26)?

Verse 27 is not trying to say we do not need teachers in the church. John himself is teaching us with this letter. According to Ephesians 4:11 one of the gifts of the Spirit is to be a teacher.

9- Twice verse 24 speaks of "abiding". What does it mean "to abide"?

"I write this to you about those who would deceive you..." (verse 26) We need that same warning today.

The liar ~ 21

4   And we are!

1 John 2:28-3:10

Again, John exhorts us to "abide in him", but this time with a condition.

1- How does Mathew 24:42-44 amplify verse 28?

2- Are we not sons of God? Don't we love our Father? Isn't Jesus our brother (Hebrews 2:12 and 17)? Why then would we avoid him in shame at his coming?

One proof that we have been born again, according to John in verse 29, is that we "do what is right". He repeats this in 3:7 and17.

3- What could he mean by "do what is right"?

John is clearly excited when he exclaims that we are children of God. What a privilege! But if we are children of God (and John emphasizes it), how can it be that the world does not recognize us? In Latin America, at least, there are many who call themselves Christians.

4- What do you think?

John states that in the world to come we will be like Christ.

5- What would "like him" be? Just how much could we be like him? Look at 2 Corinthians 3:18.

This is a great promise, but John inserts a warning. He does it by using a contrast between verses 3 and 4.

There is an important difference between some versions of the Bible in verse 4 that is repeated various times in this passage. For example, the RSV speaks of him who "commits sin" while the ESV has "makes a practice of sinning".

6- How do you understand the difference?

John doesn't say that "Jesus never sinned", but that "in him there is no sin". According to John, that deep root of sickness from where our sins sprout did not exist in him. John states that the champion of sinning is Satan. But one of the key objectives of the Lord when he came to our earth was to destroy the works of Satan.

Both the NVI and the ESV say that the true son of God does not practice sin because the "seed" of God remains in him (verse 9).

7- What "seed" could John be talking about? (There could be more than one answer.)

In one sense it is inevitable that we sin. John says it clearly in the first chapter. But to continue in sin, to continue in something that we know is not God's will, is another matter. If a person continues sinning it is a demonstration that he really does not know God. We are either sons of God or sons of the devil. There are no "gray areas" in God's kingdom. We either are sons or we are not, and our life demonstrates it. It's a matter of light or darkness, life or death.

8- As a final exercise, make a list of all the proofs that John gives that show we are true sons of God, from 1:1 to 3:10.

We cannot play games with God. We cannot have a Christian life adjusted to our personal desires. More than once I have asked myself: "How am I going to react once I am face to face with him?"

5   The assassins

1 John 3:11-24

There are themes that John repeats various times in his letter. Verse 11 is an example.

1- What reason does John offer in John 13:34, 35 that makes this message necessary?

Review the conflict between Abel and Cain in Genesis 4:3-8. Note also Hebrews 11:4.

2- What led Cain to attack his brother?

3- Note verse 13. Why would we be surprised?

Verses 13 and 15 refer to us as fellow Christians but using very strong language.

4- Is verse 14 sufficient proof that a person is of Christ? Why?

It should fill us with joy when we remember that God sent his Messiah to earth to lay down his life for us.

5- But what does it mean to "lay down our lives for our brothers"?

Verse 17 made me remember the case of a brother who was financially poor and needed a very expensive medication. He asked the church for help but their response was that they didn't have any money. But the reality was that they were spending all their funds on audio equipment. The Scriptures are very clear: the first financial responsibility of a church is to its needy members. (A brother from another church helped him).

John says that we should love our brother in Christ, that person of flesh and blood whom we know. In one sense it is easy to love "humanity", but the love that John describes isn't an ideal but something that should stimulate us to action.

Surely we have heard many times from the pulpit about the need to love our brothers in Christ.

6- Why is it, then, that we can see so many examples of the lack of love?

7- Verse 19 starts with "By this we will know..." What is "this"?

John speaks of the Christian whose heart does not condemn him (verse 20). But it is very easy for us to do wrong (either purposely or by ignorance) and still our heart does not condemn us.

I suspect that it is something many of us have felt at times. But how do we fit into this the reality that "God is greater than our hearts, and he knows everything" (RSV). Really, if God knows everything maybe it should cause concern, not relief.

8- What do you think?

Verse 22 raises a problem that has created a lot of controversy. Do we receive everything we ask? One way to clarify the question is to remember that the Bible gives us conditions and limitations to our prayers.

9- What are some of those limitations according to Mark 11:25, James 1:5-7 and 1 Peter 3:12?

10- Why are both parts of the commandment in verse 23 essential? What happens if we lack one part?

It is really great to realize that God can be in us and we in him (verse 24).

11- In what way does the Spirit let us know that?

"God is love, and he who abides in God abides in love, and God abides in him." (4:16 RSV)

28 ~ The letters of John

6 The true key

1 John 4:1-21

The world is full of "Christian" voices. Some genuine, others distorted. John insists that we must listen with discernment.

The problem that John lived with was "Gnosticism", a philosophical system that had begun to infiltrate the churches. In essence the system claimed that matter was bad and that good was spiritual. As a consequence, some denied the incarnation and denied also that Christ had come in a physical body.

1- If we denied the incarnation, what essential truths of our faith would we deny?

Note that the emphasis of John is not only concerning the content of the false message but also of its origin: if it is from God or from the devil. Because, as John has affirmed, there are other spirits, other than the Holy Spirit, that offer their message. All that is "spiritual" is not necessarily from God.

2- What could be a present-day proof that a preacher or teacher is false?

John says that they had "overcome" the false prophets (verse 4).

3- In what way may we "overcome" those who come with a false message?

John says that this is possible since "he who is in you is greater than he who is in the world." (Verse 4)

4- Who is more powerful compared with whom?

5- If the person who is not of God does not listen to us (verse 6), then what sense is there in trying to evangelize?

In verse 7 John returns to what is his central theme. He repeats it a number of times.

6- What is the difference between saying "God shows us his love" and "God is love"?

7- What is the difference between God's love and the most excellent human love?

The way God showed his love is very clear. He is the one who took the initiative (verse 19). He is the one who sent Jesus to the cross in order to give us life (verse 9). I am sure that all who say they are disciples of Jesus Christ would affirm that.

"Abide" is a strong word. It suggests consistency, stability. And it is a theme that Jesus himself affirmed (as in John 15:4).

8- In verses 13 to 16 there are three proofs that we abide in God and God in us. What are they?

9- How do you understand the last part of verse 17?

10- Verse 18 speaks of fear. What could the Christian fear?

In the last verses of chapter 4, John repeats his main theme: we must love our brothers and sisters. If we don't do it, we really don't love God.

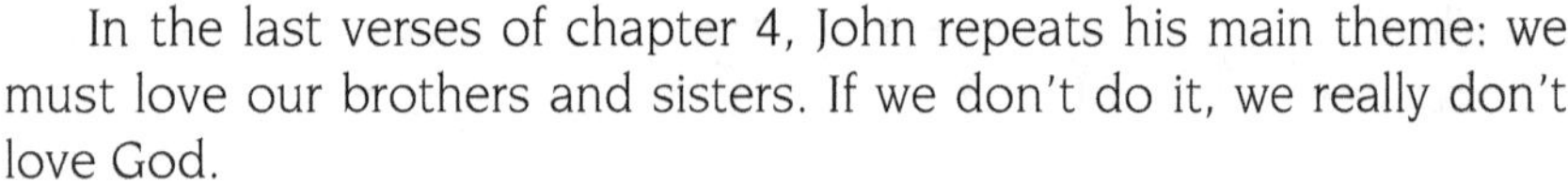

11-   But how can we love a person that we cannot tolerate?

John's message is so simple... simple yet difficult. The picture he paints is black and white... no grey areas. We can define the Christian life with one word: love. Easy to say but difficult to live.

7 The victory

1 John 5:1-12

Eight times in this letter John has used the word "believe". But, as James 2:13-20 insists, "there is faith... and there is faith".

1- For example, is it the same to say "I believe in Jesus" as to say "I believe that Jesus is the Christ"?

2- Why, according to John, is obedience the proof that our love for God is real?

3- John says that the commandments of God are not "burdensome". Has that been your experience?

4- **In verses 4 and 5 John speaks three times of "overcoming the world".**

    a) **What does it mean to "overcome the world"?**

    b) **Does John present it as an accomplishment or a challenge?**

    c) **Have you overcome the world?**

There is a variety of interpretations of the meaning of the "water and the blood" in verse 6. Without doubt this is one of the most difficult parts of John's letter. He refers again to this in verse 8.

5- **One possible explanation is that it refers to the beginning and the end of Christ's ministry. If that is so, what could they represent?**

John says that there are three witnesses to Christ: the Spirit, the water and the blood, and that they are in agreement.[1]

6- In what must they agree?

7- In what way can we call the Spirit a "witness"?

John says that what separates life from death is the Son. To have him is to have life; not to have him is death.

8- But what is "to have" the Son?

The message of John is very simple; everything depends on Jesus the Christ. With him we have everything, without him we have nothing.

1   The older versions of the King James Bible have the words "...there are three that bear record in heaven, the Father, the Word, and the Holy Ghost..." These words appear first in a manuscript in Latin in the 4th century but in no Greek manuscript until the 15th century. They were apparently added at a later date by some pious scribe.

8 Our protection

1 John 5.13-21

Some translations of the Bible have a subtitle here, but we have to always remember that the numeration of chapters and verses as well as the subtitles were added to help us in our reading and study. Verse 13 is simply the conclusion of verses 11 and 12.

But verse 14 introduces a new theme. John has already mentioned that there are conditions that must be met if we are to expect God to answer our prayer.

1- What are the conditions he mentions earlier in this letter?

John in this passage says that we must ask "according to his will" (verse 14).

2- What is the difference between asking "according to his will" and asking "if it is his will"?

3- How can we know if something we ask is according to his will or not?

In verse 16 John brings up a difficult subject. But first a review: in his letter John draws a clear line separating those who have life from those who do not.

4- What is the essential difference between the two groups of people? What is the key item that separates them?

Surely many who read verse 16 will think of Mark 3:28-30. But it is important to note two things: first, according to Jesus (Mark 3) all sin can be forgiven but one sin.

And second, we can only understand what Jesus said if we take into account the context, that is, Mark 3:30.

5- If we take into account what Mark says, what would be the only sin without forgiveness?

In this passage John mentions two classes of people: those who might sin and those who have committed the unpardonable sin.

6- What could be the reason that we should pray for the first, but not the second?

Commentators and some versions of the Bible in their notes indicate that the word "God" does not appear in the original version of the Bible in verse 16. It simply says "he will give them life..." but most translators feel that it is "obvious" that "he" must be God.

7- But if we take the original that says "...he will ask, and he will give him life...", what could John be saying if "God" is not in the verse?

There are a number of passages in the Bible that name Satan as the one who is ruling in this world (Juan 12:31, 14:30, 16:11 and Ephesians 6:12). He has been given permission to rule until Christ returns to this world.

But John states that the enemy cannot touch us. He said it already in 4:4. But what we normally say, when something bad happens (murders, car accidents, earth quakes, etc.) is that God permitted it.

8- Is that a correct way to explain the event?

In the last verses there are three things that are certain (We know…).

9- What are they?

John ends saying that we should keep ourselves from idols.

10- How does that apply to us now?

11- As a conclusion, what does John's letter teach us about:
   a) The incarnation?

   b) Sin?

   c) Love?

   d) Whether we do or do not have a life-giving relationship with God?

One of John's characteristics is that he says a lot in few words. But what he does say has to do with life and death. His purpose is clear:

"He who has the Son has life; he who has not the Son of God has not life. I write this to you who believe in the name of the Son of God, that you may know you have eternal life." (1 John 5:12, 13)

SECOND AND THIRD JOHN

Introduction

These two letters of John are the shortest books in the Bible. They would have filled one sheet of papyrus, which was the normal format for a letter. The author does not give his name, yet the commentators are in agreement that the style and content of the letters indicate John must have written it.

Both letters repeat what was one of John's main themes, and the two confront similar problems.

Second John

1- John begins his letter, as was the custom at that time, naming himself… though in this case, he did not give his actual name. a) When he refers to himself as "the elder", what does he mean? (Peter calls himself "elder" in 1 Peter 5:1). There are two possible interpretations (the commentators are not in agreement as to which is more correct).

b) How did you arrive at your decision?

John writes to an "elect lady". Here again there are two possible ways to understand the expression. The majority of the commentators feel that it refers to a church.

2- There are various references in the Old Testament that speak of Israel as the "bride" (as in Jeremiah 2:2). Can you find at least one text in the New Testament that refers to the church as a "bride" or "wife"?

John writes to a church, and it would have been a house church as they all were at that time. He said that he loved them "in the truth". He was content since he had met some members of the church and saw that they were living the truth. Though some commentators feel that verse 4 implies that there were members who were in error.

3- What would it mean to love someone "in the truth" or "because of the truth" (verse 2)?

Grace, mercy and peace (verse 3). How much they are needed in a world as convulsed as ours is. And, sadly, many churches presently are in the same condition. Also, it is important to note that verse 3 is a statement, not a request.

4- The word "truth" is repeated five times in the first four verses. What do we learn about truth?

In verse 4 John dives into the purpose of his letter. It has to do with the life of the church (verses 4-6) and the danger facing them from outside (verses 7-11).

5- The word "commandment" is repeated four times in verses 4-6. What do we learn about commandments from this?

John emphasizes love as key to the Christian life, something we saw in his first letter. But what is "love"? Is it something we feel… something we do?

6- How can a person love if he or she does not feel it?

The ESV version of the Bible is more literal in verses 4-6 when it states: "walking in the truth", "walk according to his commandments", "walk in it" (the RSV uses "follow"). The Greek word translated "walk" is a figure we often encounter in the New Testament.

7- What do we learn in these verses about our "walk"?

8- Twice in these verses John speaks of "from the beginning". What beginning?

John has emphasized the three concepts of love, truth and commandment. They are very related, and together they form the shield that protects from the error he describes in the following verses.

Beginning with verse 7 we see the purpose behind this letter. "Missionaries" of a false teaching were going around and visiting the churches.

Verses 10 and 11 reflect the traditions of the time. Since travelers had little chance of finding adequate accommodations, the churches regularly received them and offered them food and a bed. But John emphasizes an exception to that custom. It was necessary to be careful since some would come with false intentions.

And it is important to recognize that John is not speaking of persons who think differently, or even those who could possibly have doctrinal errors. The church can be a "hospital" for such people. And he is writing to a church, not to an individual. Verse 10 likely refers to a home church.

The problem is with teachers of false doctrine, especially doctrine that distorts the essence of the Gospel.

9- Could these verses have an application today?

Verse 8 warns about the danger. It was possible that the results of the work that had been done could be lost. What is not clear is whose work John is speaking about. The Greek original allows either "our" or "your", and most versions indicate both possibilities.

10- What does John mean if this verse speaks of:
a) "our work"?

b) "your work"?

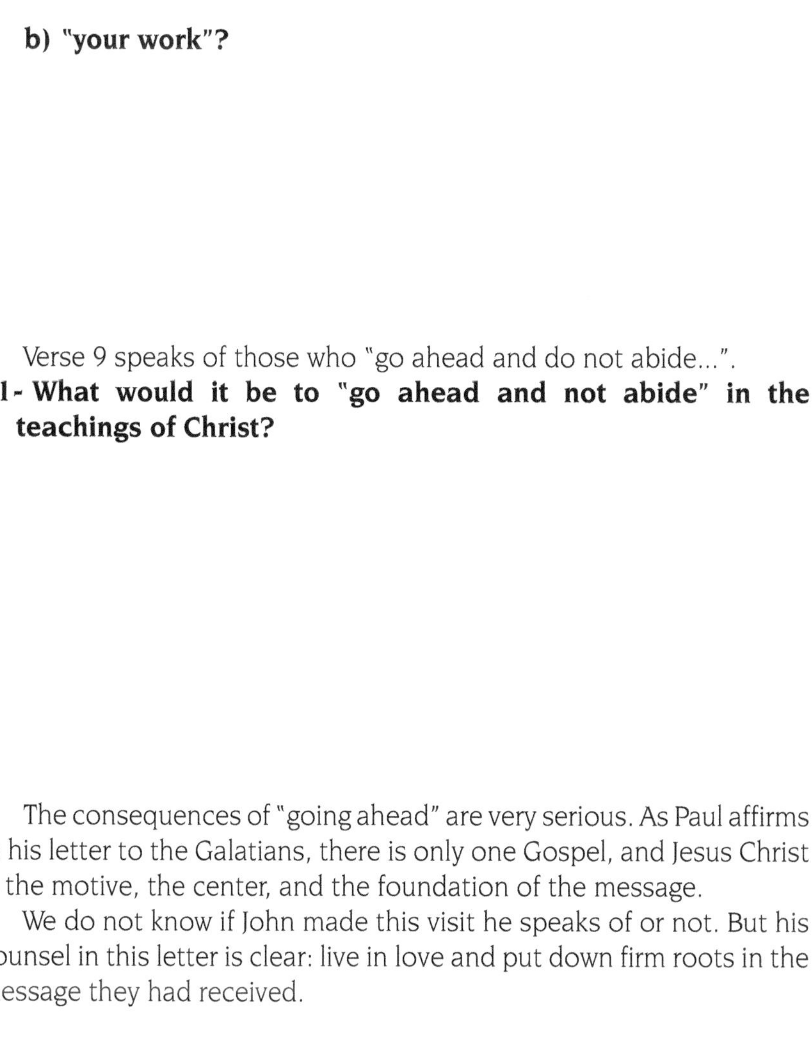

Verse 9 speaks of those who "go ahead and do not abide...".

11- What would it be to "go ahead and not abide" in the teachings of Christ?

The consequences of "going ahead" are very serious. As Paul affirms in his letter to the Galatians, there is only one Gospel, and Jesus Christ is the motive, the center, and the foundation of the message.

We do not know if John made this visit he speaks of or not. But his counsel in this letter is clear: live in love and put down firm roots in the message they had received.

Third John

John's third letter is the shortest book in the Bible. It is different from the other two letters in that it is directed to a person, Gaius. The background of the letter is roughly like this:

A group, probably from John's church, made a missionary trip. As was the norm in those days, they expected to be received by a church. But when they went to this one, probably the church of a certain Diotrephes, they were not welcomed.

1- What do we learn about Gaius in John's letter?

We can see from verse 2 that John was confident of Gaius' spiritual health.

2- Why did he have such confidence?

3- Can we apply the same reasoning to verify the spiritual health of a fellow Christian?

John was glad because his spiritual children practiced the truth.
4- What prevents a person from putting the truth in practice?

In verses 5-8 John returns to the central theme of the second letter, but here we see the other side of the issue. The churches were to be careful of false teachers and those who wanted to take advantage of them, but that did not nullify their responsibility of practicing hospitality.

The word "hospitality" is found only six times in the New Testament.
5- What do the following verses teach us about hospitality?
    a) Romans 12:13; Hebrews 13:2; 1 Peter 4:9.

    b) 1 Timothy 3:2; Titus 1:8.

We find the roots of the practice mentioned in verse 7 for the first time in the gospels.
6- Look up Mark 6:8, 9. Why would the Lord have insisted on those restrictions?

In verse 9 we encounter a person called Diotrephes. This is the only time we encounter his name in the New Testament, so we don't know anything more about him.

7- John condemned him, and it appears that there were a good six reasons why he did it. Can you find them?

Diotrephes is a good example of Christian arrogance. It happens when a brother, for various possible reasons, considers himself better than the rest.

8- Look for two or more passages in the New Testament that describe how a person who is responsible in the church should conduct themselves.

The name Demetrius is mentioned only twice in the New Testament, and it is unlikely that they be the same person. It is probable that he took the letter to Gaius and John wanted to be sure that he was well received.

9- Everyone gave good testimony about Gaius and John said that even the truth testified about him. How can the truth testify about a person?

John again says that he had much more to say, but that he preferred to do it personally. And with that, he closes with greetings.

How to use this study

These studies are study guides, that is, their purpose is to guide you in your personal study of the subject or book of the Bible that the guide develops.

What the study proposes is a discussion. We introduce the theme, suggest how to proceed with the investigation, we comment, but we also ask. The spaces after the questions are for you to write in your answers.

We are hoping that with this give and take we help you to build your own understanding of the material. Not second hand, as when you listen to a sermon, but as fruit of your own reading and investigation.

How to do the study?

1 – Before you start, pray. Ask God that he might speak to you and give you understanding during your study.

2 – When there is a Bible passage, read it more than one time and ask yourself: What is the writer trying to say? Even though many use the King James version of the Bible it would be good to have other versions available, so you can compare scripture with scripture. The Revised Standard Version, the New International Version or others can help you see the passage of scripture with more clarity.

3 – Do the lesson. Try your best to make as clear an answer as possible. Don't hurry just to finish. It is better to go carefully, thinking, asking, clarifying.

With the group

Personal study is important, but its value increases if it is accompanied with study in a group. A group of up to 8 people is ideal, but if the group is only you and one other person it is still better than studying alone.

Actually these studies have been designed with this purpose: to stimulate the study of the Bible in small groups. The system to use is simple:

1 – **Do one of the chapters on your own**. Even if there are things you don't understand, do your best to finish the chapter.

2 – **Meet with the group**. In the group you share the answers to each question. It is very possible that you will not all have the same answers, but then by comparing the results among the entire group you can clarify and if necessary correct your answer.

It is the discussion above all that provides the greatest benefit of this system of study.

3 – **Avoid getting off the subject**. It is easy to get distracted by personal issues or arguments about some particular question. If an important issue comes up you can dedicate a special session of the group to handle it.

4 – **Participate**. Everyone should take part. It is that which gives value to the study in group.

5 – **Listen**. We often have the tendency to jump in with our own conclusions before we allow the other person to finish. We will learn from each other, even from those, who in our opinion, are wrong.

6 – **Don't dominate the discussion**. It may be that you have the study down pat, yet it is important that you give space to others and encourage the possibly timid person to take part.

May the Lord help you in this task, and if you need help we are ready to assist you. Feel free to contact us.